CONTENTS

Introduction

Making things with brown paper bags and cardboard tubes is a great way to keep little hands busy and encourage creativity. Toys, animals, puppets, gifts, holiday fare all take shape with a minimum of effort and no special equipment. These simple projects are fun to do and they can be worked on by individuals or groups with parent or teacher guiding the way. Even preschoolers can share in these activities.

Save the tubes from gift paper, toilet tissue rolls, wax paper/plastic wrap rolls and collect various sizes of brown paper bags from grocery and department stores. Bags can be stuffed with old newspapers and glued and painted to make all sorts of interesting and amazing projects for children to play with or use at home or school.

Some of the projects in this book such as napkin rings, place mats and paperweights, trick or treat bags, footballs, kites, and Christmas tree decorations have practical applications. Others are great for make-believe if you're creating a play and need puppets or costumes, or you want to wear a mask.

You and your children will enjoy all of these projects. Make them on a rainy day when the children can't go out to play or use them for classroom creative activities. Children love the hands-on approach and even little ones can't spoil expensive paper or tools because everything needed to make these projects is easy to replace—usually free. Children can experiment for their own special creation. A little paint or paper and glue can add a different touch and the projects are so easy to do that each item is always successful. Projects can look spectacular simply by adding a paper doily, a paper bow, sparkles, or buttons. You and your children will spend many happy hours making and using these projects. Remember to observe some basic safety rules—have small children use blunt-nose scissors and make eye holes in masks so that vision is not obstructed.

If you appreciate that trees from our forests are used to make paper and in turn, paper bags, you'll feel satisfied to know that recycling the bags into these delightful toys and crafts gives the paper a longer life.

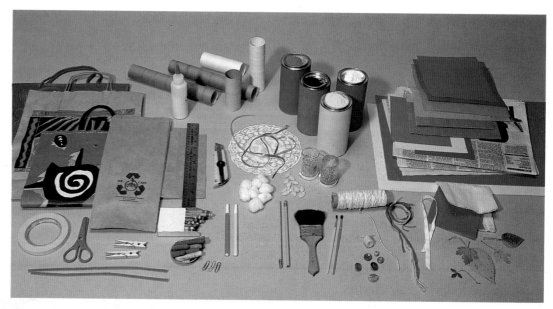

Fun with Paper Bags & Cardboard Tubes
●■▲
F. Virginia Walter

A Sterling/Tamos Book

Sterling Publishing Co., Inc.   New York

A Sterling/Tamos Book
First paperback edition published in 1994 by
Sterling Publishing Company, Inc.
387 Park Avenue South, New York, N.Y. 10016

TAMOS Books Inc.
300 Wales Avenue, Winnipeg, MB, Canada R2M 2S9

© 1992 by F. Virginia Walter
Distributed in Canada by Sterling Publishing
% Canadian Manda Group, P.O. Box 920, Station U
Toronto, Ontario, Canada M8Z 5P9
Distributed in Great Britain and Europe by Cassell PLC
Villiers House, 41/47 Strand, London WC2N 5JE, England
Distributed in Australia by Capricorn Link (Australia) Pty Ltd.
P.O. Box 6651, Baulkham Hills, Business Centre, NSW 2153, Australia

Projects and illustrations Teddy Cameron Long
Photography Walter Kaiser, Custom Images Ltd., Wpg
Design A. O. Osen

Library of Congress Cataloging-in-Publication Data
Walter, F. Virginia
    Fun with paper bags & cardboard tubes/ by F.Virginia Walter
[illustrations by Teddy Cameron Long].
        p.   cm.
    Includes index.
    ISBN 1-895569-08-7
    1. Paper work. 2. Paper bags.   I. Title.   II. Title: Fun with paper
bags and cardboard tubes.
TT870.W288   1992
745.54 - - dc20   92-14944
                                                           CIP

Canadian Cataloging-in-Publication Data
    Walter, F. Virginia, 1935-
    Fun with paper bags & cardboard tubes
    "A Sterling/Tamos Book."
    ISBN 1-895569-08-7
I. Paper work. II. Title.
TT870.W34 1992   745.54   C92-098041-4

10 9 8 7 6 5 4 3 2 1

Sterling ISBN 1-895569-08-7 Trade
                1-895569-26-5 Paper

The advice and directions given in this book have been carefully checked, prior to printing, by the Author as well as the Publisher. Nevertheless, no guarantee can be given as to project outcome due to possible differences in material and the Author and Publisher will not be responsible for the results.

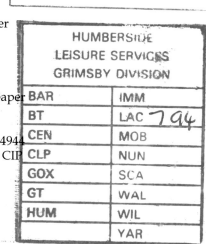

TOYS & GAMES

Paper Bag Kite

Cut an upright thin stick or dowel 24 in (61cm) long. Cut the cross dowel 18 in (46cm) long. Place the short dowel across the long one, 9 in (23cm) from the top. Glue. Lash the join with several windings of strong cord. Allow to dry.

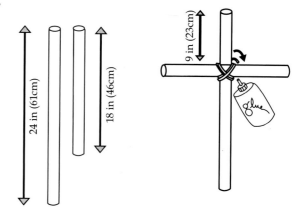

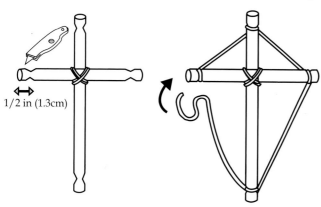

Measure 1/2 in (1.3cm) from the ends of each dowel, and make a small cut all the way around the dowel. Run some string around the notch and down to other notches to form the outline of the kite, as shown.

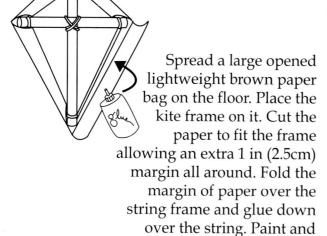

Spread a large opened lightweight brown paper bag on the floor. Place the kite frame on it. Cut the paper to fit the frame allowing an extra 1 in (2.5cm) margin all around. Fold the margin of paper over the string frame and glue down over the string. Paint and decorate.

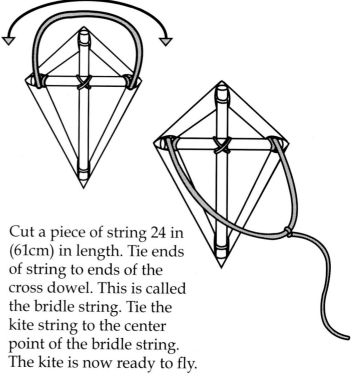

Cut a piece of string 24 in (61cm) in length. Tie ends of string to ends of the cross dowel. This is called the bridle string. Tie the kite string to the center point of the bridle string. The kite is now ready to fly.

Flying Fish Kite

Cut the bottom out of a brown paper bag. Cut down one side to make a flat sheet. Fold under 1 in (2.5cm) along one side of bag and place piece of string under fold, allowing 24 in (61cm) of string to hang free on one side. Glue down fold. Glue 2 short ends together to form a cylinder, with string hanging out at top.

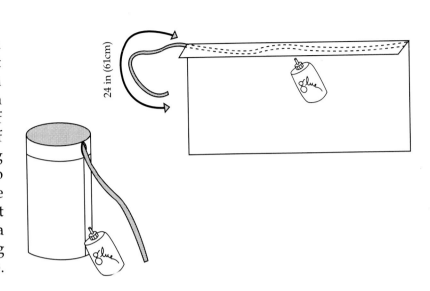

Cut out fins from another paper bag and glue on fish. Paint on eyes, scales, gills, and tail, as shown. Cut an upright thin stick or dowel 24 in (61cm) long. Tie strings to end of dowel. Fish will fly in wind. If kite swivels too much in wind, add 2 more short strings to each side of fish kite mouth, as shown in photograph.

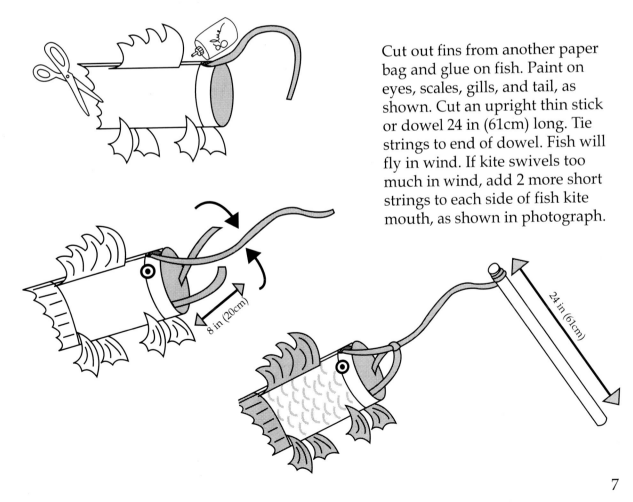

Football

Lightly stuff a brown paper lunch bag with crumpled newspaper until almost full.

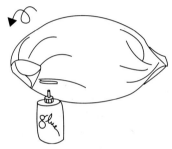

Spread glue around the inside edge of the open end and twist closed. Twist bottom end, as shown, to form a football shape and spread glue in the creases. Twist again.

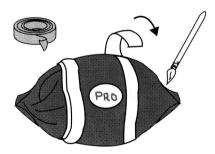

Wrap masking tape around each end, approximately 2 in (5cm) from tips, as shown. Allow to dry. Paint brown with crest on front of ball.

8

Badminton
Racket

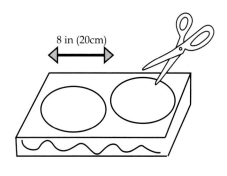

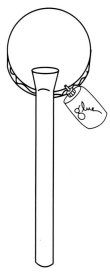

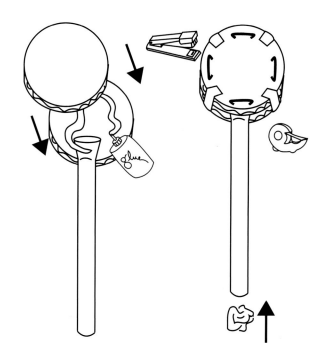

Cut 2 circles of thick cardboard each 8 in (20cm) in diameter. Glue a long cardboard tube to the back of one circle, as shown.

Flatten the cardboard tube against the cardboard circle. Spread glue over the back of the circle and part of tube that touches circle. Place second circle on top of the glue.

Tape and staple the 2 circles together. Stuff the remainder of the tube tightly with newspaper for strength. Paint and shellac racket and birdie.

Birdie

To make birdie, cut a 4 in (10cm) square of brown paper. Spread glue over one side of square and roll into a cone, glue side inward. Squeeze a bit of glue inside the tip of the cone. Crumple a tiny piece of newspaper 3 in (7.6cm) square, and push into tip of cone to weight the cone nose.

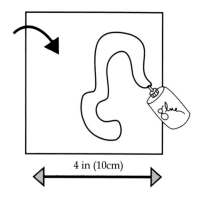

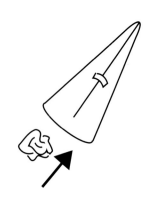

10

Hockey
Stick

Use a long cardboard tube from giftwrap. Fold one end 6 in (15cm) up from the end of tube. Glue the folds and tape until dry. Tape well with black electrician's tape around the folded end, as shown. Stuff tube tightly with crumpled newspaper for added strength. Paint the stick and put your favorite team's emblem on the side of the stick. Shellac.

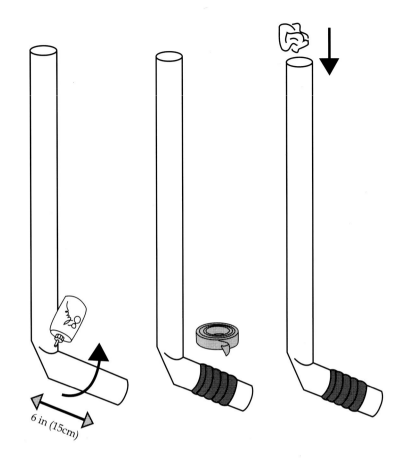

6 in (15cm)

Puck

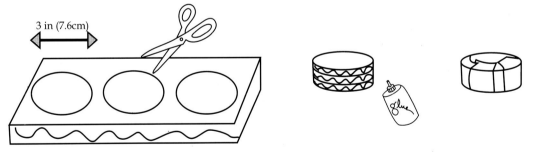

3 in (7.6cm)

To make puck, draw 3 circles, 3 in (7.6cm) in diameter on thick cardboard.

Cut out and glue one on top of the other. Cover the edges with small pieces of brown paper and glue, as shown. Paint. Allow to dry. Shellac.

Toss Game

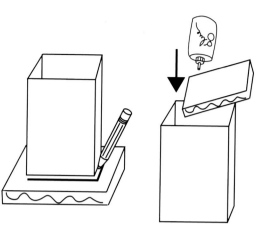

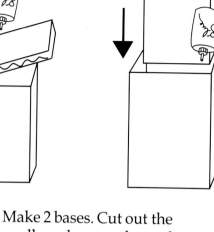

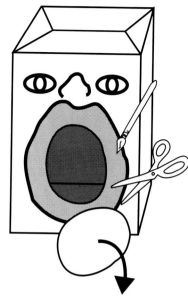

You will need 2 brown paper grocery bags the same size. Set one open bag on a piece of heavy cardboard and trace around the base.

Make 2 bases. Cut out the cardboard rectangles and glue one to the inside bottom of each bag. Place one open end into the other bag, gluing the sides well. Allow to dry.

Draw a clown face with a wide open mouth on the front of the bag. Cut out the mouth area. Paint.

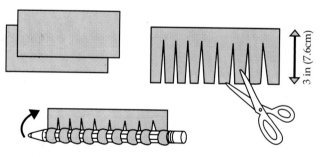

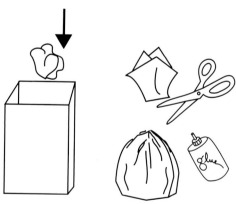

To make clown hair, cut out the sides of another brown paper grocery bag. Paint it orange. When dry shellac. Cut the paper in strips 3 in (7.6cm) wide. Fringe each strip along the long side and curl the fringe around a pencil. Glue strips to the top of the toss game bag, as shown.

To make balls for toss game, crumple one sheet of news-paper and place it in a lunch bag. Cut off excess bag and glue bag shut. Paint and shellac. Make several. Toss into open mouth.

Pan Pipes

Cut 4 or 5 cardboard tubes into different lengths, each 1 in (2.5cm) longer than the last. Cut each tube down one side, as shown.

Add glue to cut edges and overlap, making each tube 1 in (2.5cm) in diameter. Tape in place until the glue dries.

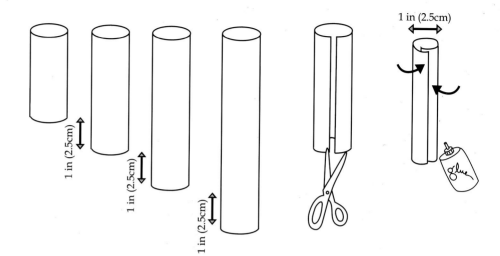

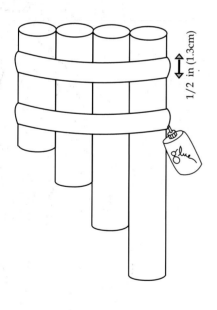

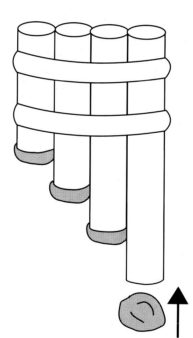

Lay the tubes in a row, from shortest to longest, even at the top. Glue the tubes together and tape. Glue thin cardboard strips 1/2 in (1.3cm) wide across the tubes for extra support.

Paint and decorate. When dry, shellac. Roll up balls of plasticine slightly larger than the openings of the tube, and plug the bottom of each tube. Blow across the open tops to play.

14

Circus Train

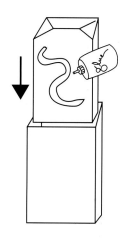

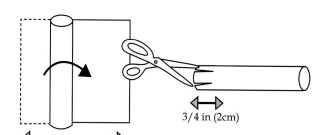

5 in (13cm)

3/4 in (2cm)

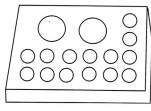

Use 8 small brown paper lunch bags. For a strong train, spread glue over outside of one bag and slip into another bag, open end in. Make 4.

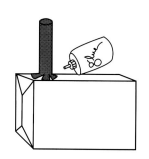

Cut a piece of brown paper 5 in (13cm) square and roll into a tube. Glue edge and make 4 — 3/4 in (2cm) cuts around one end. Glue cut tabs to top of engine bag.

From thick cardboard, cut 2 large wheels and 14 small wheels for the engine and

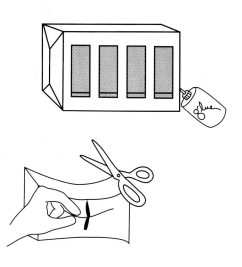

Cut slits in sides of 3 bags for animal cages. Pinch in center of sides to start cutting slits. Glue the double layer of bars together for added strength.

16

cars. Paint black. When dry glue wheels to engine, as shown. To make cowcatcher, cut a triangle 6 in (15cm) high. Make a 1 in (2.5cm) cut in center of base. Fold one flap over the other and glue,

as shown. Paint with black stripes. When dry, glue to front of engine, as shown.

Cut window for an engineer. Draw top half of clown on brown paper. Cut out and paint. Glue inside the window of engine. Paint cars and

engine with crayons and pencils. Add glitter. Glue remaining wheels to the animal cars. Join animal cars together with strips of brown paper. Cut out circus animals from brown paper and paint to resemble the animals. Glue them inside the boxcars.

Mystery Bags

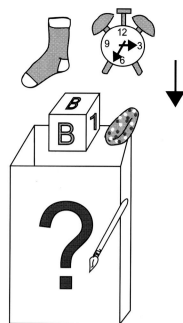

Use brown paper lunch bags. Decorate each bag with paint, crayons, or chalk to suit the event. For example, fill one bag with various shapes and colors for a touch-and-tell bag.

Fill another with different stones for a discussion bag, and another with items that rhyme for a rhyme bag. Or you could make a Valentine bag or a numbers bag.

X-ray Spyglass

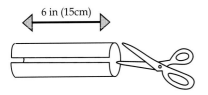

6 in (15cm)

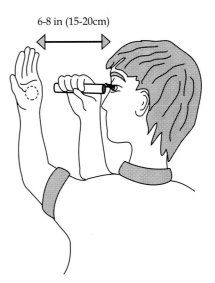

6-8 in (15-20cm)

1 in (2.5cm)

Cut a length of cardboard tube 6 in (15cm) long. Cut down one side and add glue to one edge, overlap edges, making tube about 1 in (2.5cm) in diameter. Tape in place until glue dries. Paint and shellac.

Hold tube up to one eye. Hold other open hand about 6 to 8 in (15 to 20cm) in front of other end of tube. Both eyes remain open. There will appear to be a hole in your hand that you can see through.

19

Fans

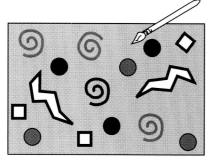

Cut out the side of a brown paper grocery bag. Paint and decorate one side. Allow to dry.

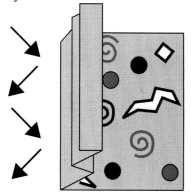

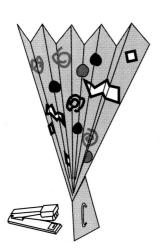

Accordion pleat fan in 1 in (2.5cm) folds. Staple one end, as shown.

Pinwheels

Cut a 6 in (15cm) square from a brown paper bag. Make a cut from each corner 2/3 of the way to the center point, as shown. Paint the triangular shapes different colors, back and front. Allow to dry. Shellac.

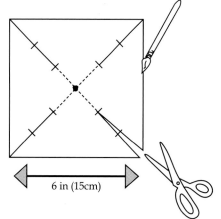

6 in (15cm)

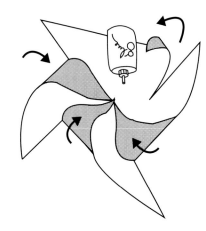

Bring every other point to the center, as shown, and glue.

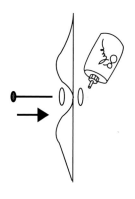

Make 2 small circles of brown paper for washers and glue on either side of the pinwheel at the center point. Push a straight pin through the center point before the glue dries.

Push pin into the eraser on a pencil. Look at the drawings to see the effect of placing the pin into the pencil eraser at different angles. Blow on the pinwheel to turn.

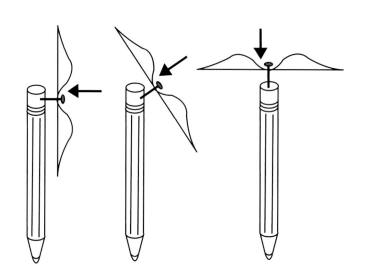

Pop-up Puppets

Bug in Flower

Cut out flower and 2 leaves from thin cardboard and paint flower pink and leaves green. Glue to front of toilet tissue tube.

From thin cardboard cut out bug shape with legs. Bend legs down. Paint, as shown p25.

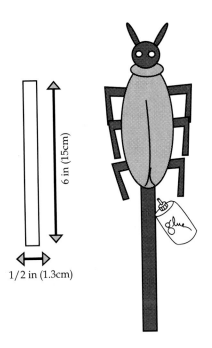

6 in (15cm)

1/2 in (1.3cm)

Cut out cardboard strip 6 in long and 1/2 in wide (15cm x 1.3cm) and paint black. When dry glue bug to strip. Insert bug in flower tube. Hold strip to make bug move up and down.

Chicken in Egg

Cut one end of toilet tissue tube into points to look like a cracked egg.

Cut an egg shape from thin cardboard. Glue to tube. Paint white.

 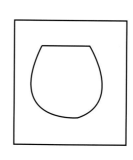 

From thin cardboard, cut out chick head and paint, as shown p25. Cut out cardboard strip 6 in long and 1/2 in wide (15cm x 1.3cm) and paint yellow. When dry glue chick head to strip. Move strip up and down inside tube.

 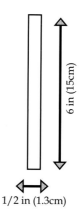

6 in (15cm)

1/2 in (1.3cm)

Jack-in-the-Box

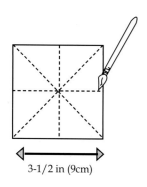

3-1/2 in (9cm)

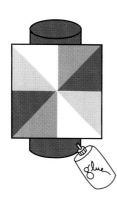 

6 in (15cm)

1/2 in (1.3cm)

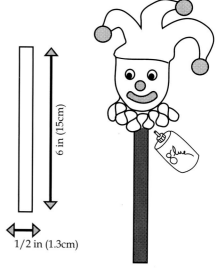

Cut out a 3-1/2 in (9cm) thin cardboard square and paint, as shown. Glue to front of toilet tissue tube.

On thin cardboard draw a

face shape with jester hat and ruffle. Cut out. Paint face and hat, as shown p25. Cut one piece of cardboard strip 6 in (15cm) long and 1/2 in (1.3cm) wide. Paint black.

When dry glue jester head to strip. Move strip up and down inside tube.

Toy Chest

Cut down one side of the front of a brown paper grocery bag and across the bottom, as shown. Fold the front flap back. Repeat with a second bag. Glue one bag inside the other, open ends together.

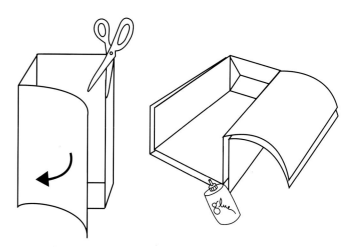

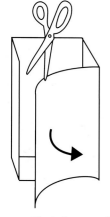

Cut down the other side of the front of a grocery bag, as shown, and across the bottom in the same way. Fold flap back. Repeat with another bag and glue together in the same way.

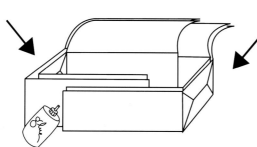

Lay one double bag flat with the flap at the back, open side up. Spread glue over the inside of the double bag. Press the second double bag into the first with the flap at the back and the open side up so that it forms a box with a

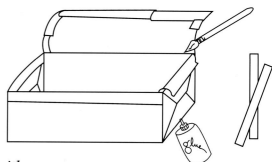

lid, as shown. Smooth together.

Cover all the cut edges with pieces of brown paper and glue to give a finished edge. Paint and shellac.

Sea Snake

Cut a cardboard tube along the seam line from end to end, as shown. Make another cut along the same line 1/2 in (1.3cm) away from the first cut, making a curled strip 1/2 in (1.3cm) wide.

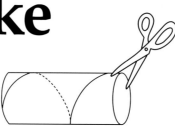

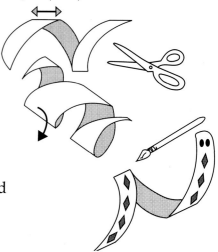

Cut one end to form a rounded head. Paint and shellac. See cover photograph.

Snail

Cut a strip 4 in (10cm) wide from the length of a brown paper bag. Fold in half lengthwise. Spread glue along one folded side, as shown. Roll tightly. Cut out a snail face from smooth cardboard. Glue face to snail body. Paint. See cover photograph.

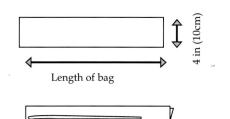

Length of bag

4 in (10cm)

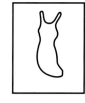

Fish

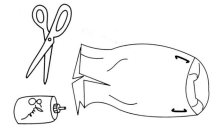

Stuff a brown paper lunch bag with crumpled newspaper. Fold the base of the paper bag inwards. Staple at sides, as shown. This serves as the fish mouth.

Cut the open end of bag in a tail shape and glue ends together to close bag. Cut out fins from another brown paper bag and glue to fish body.

Fringe the fins and tail. Paint. Suspend from a string, glued to fish. See cover photograph.

Cylinder Shaker

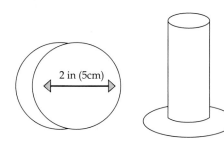

2 in (5cm)

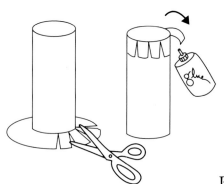

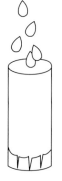

Cut 2 circles 2 in (5cm) in diameter from a heavy paper bag. Glue one end of a toilet tissue tube to the center of one circle. Allow to dry.

Make small cuts in the paper circle all around the tube. Glue circle tabs to tube.

Place several seeds inside the tube and glue the second circle to this end, as before. Paint. Allow to dry. Shellac.

28

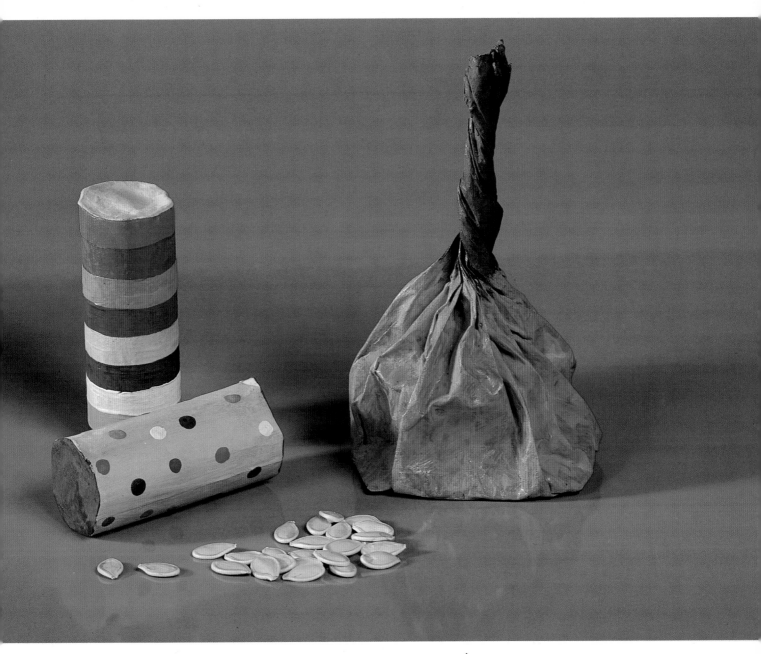

Pumpkin Shaker

Place a handful of dried pumpkin seeds in a brown paper lunch bag. Twist the opening closed, as shown. Paint. Allow to dry. Shellac.

Storage Bags

Spread glue inside a brown paper grocery bag on the bottom only. Put another grocery bag inside the first bag and press against the bottom. Drizzle glue between the sides of the bags, and press together. Fold the top 2 in (5cm) of the bags down on the outside, as shown, and glue in place. Paint each child's name on the front of his/her bag and decorate.

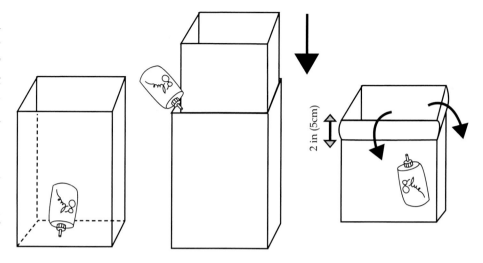

Book

Cut the bottom out of 5 brown paper grocery bags. Slit open and lay flat.

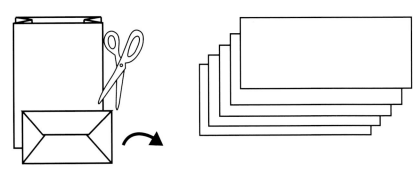

Spread glue on one sheet and lay another on top of it, making a double sheet. Smooth out. Lay all sheets on top of each other with double sheet on bottom.

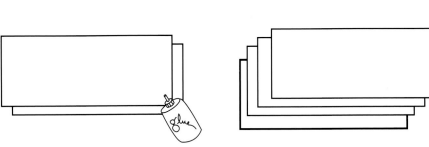

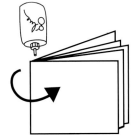

Fold, short ends together. Unfold. Run a bead of glue along the fold lines of each sheet and place sheets together. Do not put glue on top sheet.

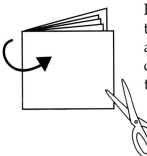

Fold book again, along the glue line. Trim pages, and cover, leaving the cover a little larger than the pages.

31

Bookends

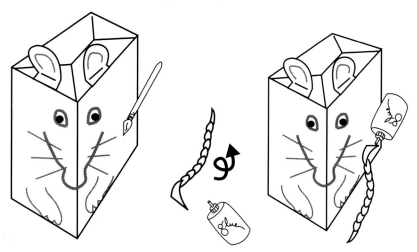

Turn a lunch bag upside down. Paint and shellac. If making an animal bookend or doorstop, cut out ears

from brown paper and glue on. Paint. For a tail spread glue over a strip of brown paper and twist into a "rat"

tail, or wrap the strip around crumpled newspaper for a fatter "cat" tail. Paint as required.

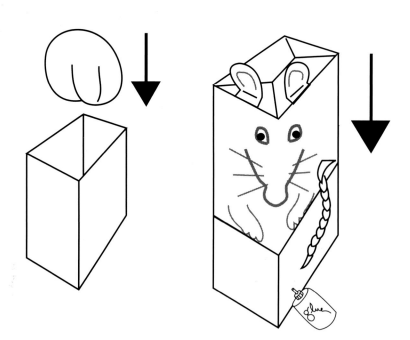

Place a heavy weight in another lunch bag and slide the painted bag over the top. Glue bags together.

Picture Frames

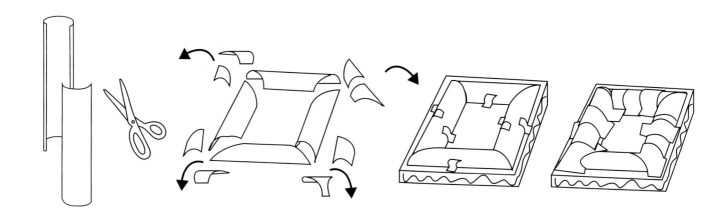

Cut 2 cardboard tubes in half lengthwise. Cut ends at an angle and fit together. Place the tubes, cut side down, on a piece of thick cardboard.

Tape in place. Cover with pieces of brown paper and glue, taking care to cover the joins well. Wrap the paper and glue right down onto the

cardboard. Trim excess cardboard and cover cut edges with more paper and glue. Paint and shellac.

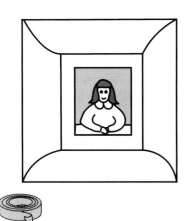

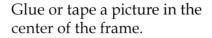

Glue or tape a picture in the center of the frame.

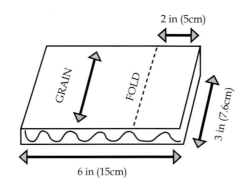

2 in (5cm)

GRAIN

FOLD

3 in (7.6cm)

6 in (15cm)

Cut another piece of thick cardboard 6 in (15cm) long and 3 in (7.6cm) wide. Cut across the grain of the cardboard, as shown.

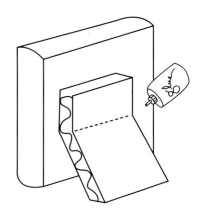

Fold 2 in (5cm) of one end over and glue the folded end to the back of the frame, about 4 in (10cm) from the bottom. This is the stand.

Hand Puppets

Lizard

Fold the base of a brown paper lunch bag inward and staple at the sides to form a mouth. Paint inside of mouth pink.

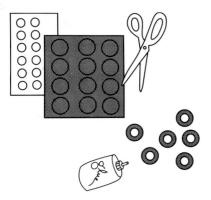

Cut out several large circles from blue construction paper and several smaller circles from yellow construction paper. Glue yellow circles on top of blue circles.

Glue circles all over lizard body, as shown.

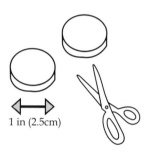

1 in (2.5cm)

Cut out 2 cardboard circles 1 in (2.5 cm) in diameter and paint as eyes.

When dry glue to lizard head. Paint lips red.

Frog Puppet

Fold the base of a brown paper lunch bag inward and staple at the sides to form a mouth.

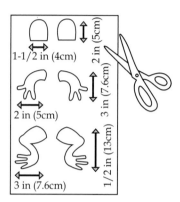

2 in (5cm)

1-1/2 in (4cm)

2 in (5cm)

3 in (7.6cm)

2 in (5cm)

3 in (7.6cm)

1/2 in (13cm)

3 in (7.6cm)

On another brown paper bag draw and cut 2 big frog eyes. Fold the eyes at the base to

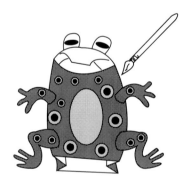

From the same brown paper bag draw and cut out front and back legs, as shown. Glue in place. Paint frog green with light green spots with black centers. Allow to dry.

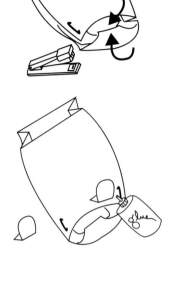

stand up and glue folded part on the top of the head. Paint yellow with black pupils.

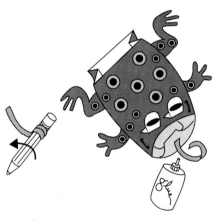

Cut a 2 in x 1/2 in (5cm x 1.3cm) piece of red construction paper and curl it around a pencil for the tongue. Paint inside of mouth red. Glue tongue to the center of the mouth.

Parrot Puppet

Fold the base of a brown paper lunch bag inward and staple at the sides to form a mouth. Paint mouth end and inside orange for a beak.

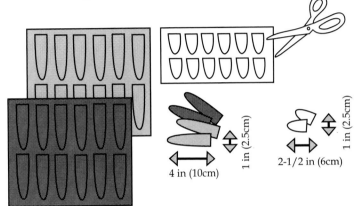

Cut out a number of strips 4 in long and 1 in wide (10cm x 2.5 cm) from green and red construction paper. Round off ends. These are feathers.

4 in (10cm)

1 in (2.5cm)

2-1/2 in (6cm)

1 in (2.5cm)

Glue green feathers around open end of bag, bottom row first and each succeeding row overlapping the other. Then, glue 2 red rows around middle of bag.

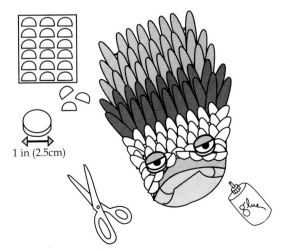

1 in (2.5cm)

From yellow construction paper cut out shorter strips 2-1/2 in long and 1 in (6cm x 2.5cm) wide. Round off ends. Glue in rows to cover rest of bag to the beak. Cut several yellow small half circles and glue near parrot beak, as shown. Cut out 2 cardboard circles 1 in (2.5cm) in diameter. Paint for eyes. When dry, glue to parrot head.

Rabbit Mask

Use a brown paper grocery bag. Cut eyeholes and flap for a nose in bottom of bag, as shown.

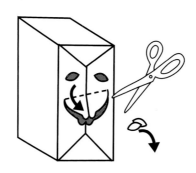

Cut out the narrow side of the bag for the child's neck, as shown.

Cut the ears from the folds on the top side of the bag, and fold forward.

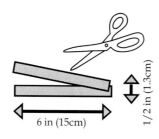

6 in (15cm)

1/2 in (1.3cm)

Cut strips of paper 1/2 in x 6 in (1.3cm x 15cm). Glue on face for whiskers. Paint and shellac.

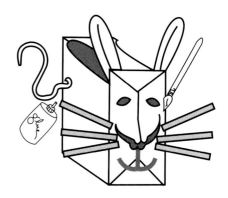

Glue strings to the open side of the bag to hold mask on, as shown.

Mouse Mask

Use the same technique as for rabbit mask, but cut rounded ears. Paint mouse face.

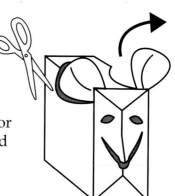

Hairy Monster

Tear a large brown paper grocery bag into strips from the open end to the base. Cut a hole in the base for the head. No arm holes are needed. Tear a smaller bag in the same way. This will cover head. Child's eyes look through the torn strips. For thick "fur," tear another 2 bags into strips and glue strips to the first 2 bags.

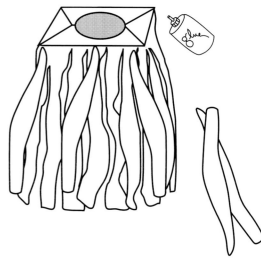

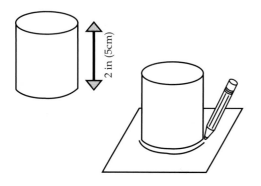

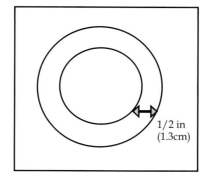

1/2 in (1.3cm)

To make eyes for the monster, cut a toilet tissue tube into 2 — 2 in (5cm) slices. Stand the end of the tube on brown paper and trace around it. Draw another circle 1/2 in (1.3cm) larger around the first circle and cut out.

Make several cuts around the edge of larger circle to the smaller circle, as shown. Glue to end of tube and glue tabs down onto sides of tube. Repeat to cover both ends of both tubes.

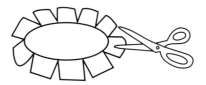

Glue tubes to front of head bag. Paint eyes on the end.

Dinosaur Costume

Use a large brown paper grocery bag for the body bag and cut a hole in the base for the head. Cut slits front and back if necessary to fit over head, as shown. Cut armholes in the sides.

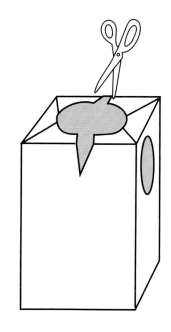

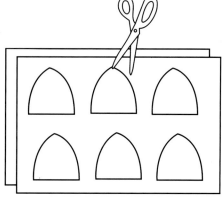

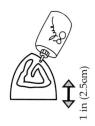

1 in (2.5cm)

Draw and cut spikes from 2 sheets of brown paper, as shown. Spread glue on 6 spikes leaving 1 in (2.5 cm) at base without glue. Attach to other 6 spikes, as shown. Fold each side of unglued bottom up.

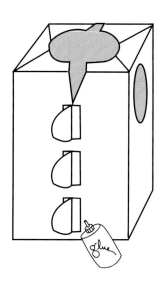

Glue 3 of these flaps to the back of body bag, as shown. Paint and shellac, as shown p43.

Make a bag for the head the same as for frog headdress (p46). Add the other 3 spikes to top and back of dinosaur headdress. Paint and shellac.

Turkey Headdress

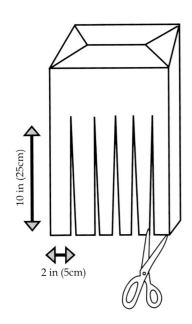

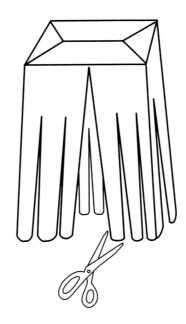

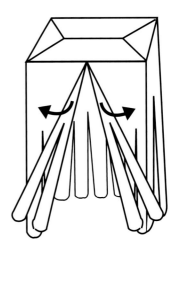

Use a large brown paper grocery bag. Cut 10 in (25cm) fringes 2 in (5cm) wide all around the opening of the bag.

Round ends of fringes. Cut the bag up the center front, as shown.

Fold back on each side and glue.

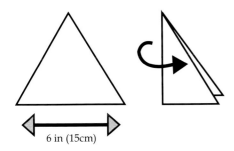

From another bag, cut a triangle with 6 in (15cm) sides, as shown. Fold it exactly in half. Paint it yellow for the beak. Allow to dry.

Glue it with the point at the front of bag, as shown. Paint fringes with black strokes to resemble turkey feathers. Paint head of turkey red with yellow and black eyes. Shellac when dry.

Frog Headdress

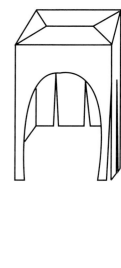

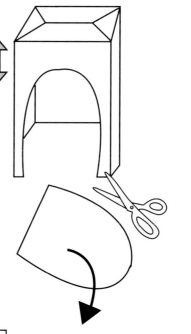

Cut an arch shape out of the wide side of a brown paper grocery bag. Cut from the open end to within 3 in (7.6cm) of the base of the bag. Cut 6 evenly spaced slits up from the bag opening about 12 in (30cm) so that bag will fit over shoulders.

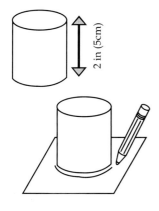

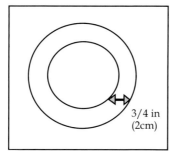

Cut 2–2 in (5cm) rings from a cardboard tube. Cover the end of each with a circle of brown paper, 3/4 in (2cm) wider than the tube rings.

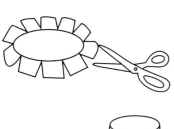

Make cuts around this circle of paper. Glue cut ends to tube rings.

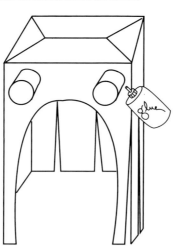

Glue rings to front of bag for eyes.

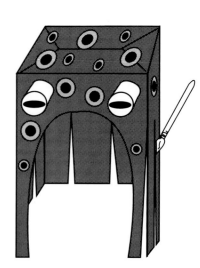

Paint the bag green with light green and black spots. Paint eyes yellow with black pupils.

Peanut Costume

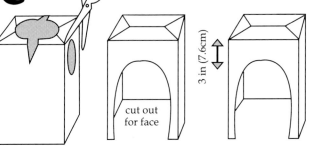

BODY BAG

HEAD BAG

3 in (7.6cm)

cut out for face

Use 3 brown paper grocery bags for costume: one for body bag (see dinosaur, p44) and 2 for head covering. Wet one head bag with a sponge, and spread glue on the inside.

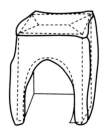

Place the dry head bag inside the wet head bag. Crumple the bag into vertical creases and set aside to dry.

Cut off the bottom of a fourth brown paper grocery bag and slit down side to open into a flat sheet. Wet this sheet with a sponge. Spread glue on one side and attach to the body bag, crumpling it into vertical creases.

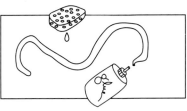

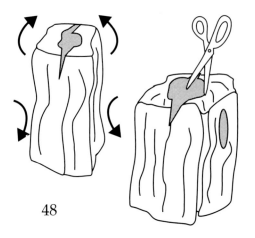

Crumple the whole bag slightly and set aside to dry. When dry, pull it open again. Cut out arm holes in second layer, and paint and shellac head and body bags.

48

Toothpaste Tube

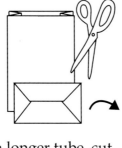

Make a plain tube body bag as in dinosaur (p44) from a brown paper grocery bag.

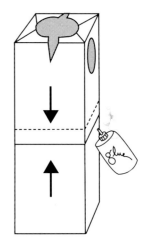

To make a longer tube, cut off the bottom of another grocery bag, and glue this bag to the bottom of the first body bag, as shown. Paint a toothpaste label on the front.

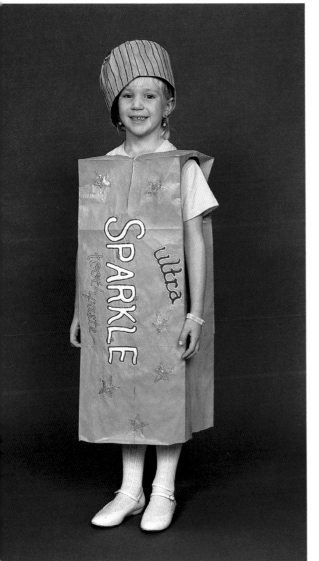

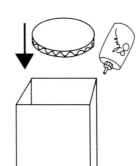

To make cap, find a brown paper bag that fits child's head. Cut a cardboard circle to fit inside the bag and glue to the bottom of the inside of the bag.

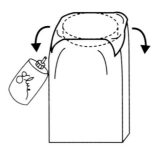

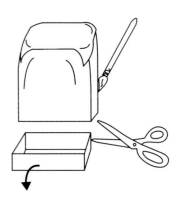

Fold down the corners of the bottom of the bag and glue. Trim open end to fit. Paint and shellac. Cap sits on head as hat.

Mirror

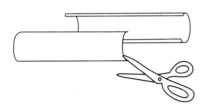

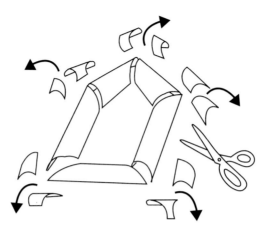

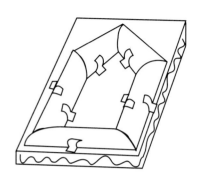

Cut 2 cardboard tubes in half lengthwise. Arrange and cut the halves in shape

of mirror, as shown. Cut the ends at an angle so that the ends fit together.

Place the tubes, curved side up, on a piece of thick cardboard. Tape in place.

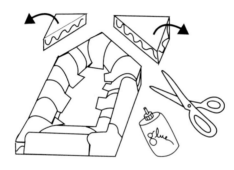

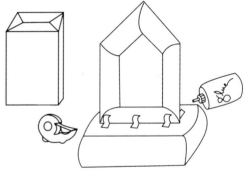

Cover with pieces of brown paper and glue, taking care to cover the joins well. Wrap the paper and glue right down onto the cardboard.

Trim excess cardboard and cover cut edges with more paper and glue. Allow to dry.

Stuff a brown paper lunch bag tightly with crumpled

newspaper. Fold the opening closed and glue shut. Lay the bag flat and glue the frame upright on the bag. Tape in place until glue dries. Paint and shellac.

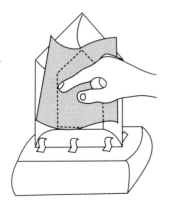

Cut piece of tinfoil a bit larger than the mirror space at center. Press in place. Run your finger around the edges.

Remove tinfoil and trim with scissors around the fold marks. Glue in place for mirror.

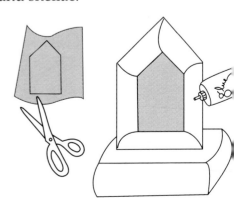

Comb

Cut 4 pieces of brown paper
5 in x 2 in (13cm x 5cm). Glue
one on top of the other. Cut
1-1/2 in (4cm) notches out of
one long side, as shown.
Paint with latex house paint
or acrylic paint.

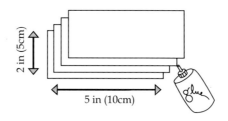

2 in (5cm)

5 in (10cm)

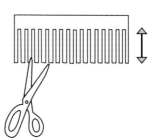

1-1/2 in (4cm)

51

Birthday Cake

Use 3 brown paper bags of different sizes. Stuff with crumpled newspaper (and treats if desired). Fold tops closed and glue. Stack bags with largest on bottom and smallest on top. Glue in place.

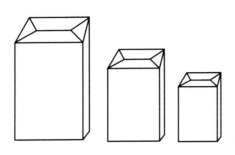

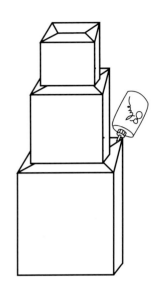

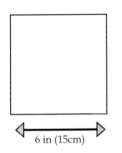 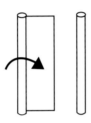

6 in (15cm)

Cut 6 in (15cm) squares of brown paper and roll each very tightly. Glue.

Poke holes in the top bag and glue the tight tubes into the holes.

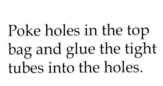

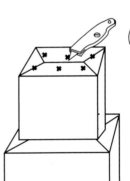

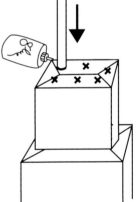

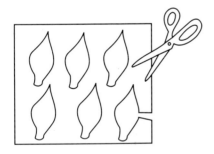

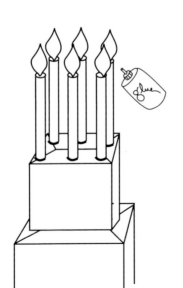

Cut flame shapes from shiny gold paper, twist the bottom and glue into the tops of the "candles." Paint cake to resemble icing. Cake may be cut open to retrieve treats or small gifts.

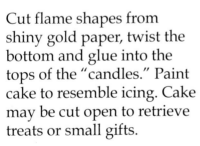

Firecracker

Cover toilet tissue tube with red paper and glue.

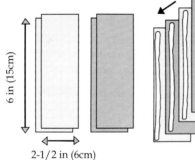

Cut 2 pieces of yellow crepe paper 6 in x 2-1/2 in (15cm x 6cm). Repeat for 2 pieces of red crepe paper.

Spread glue along one side of each piece of crepe paper as you place one color on top of the other in alternate layers.

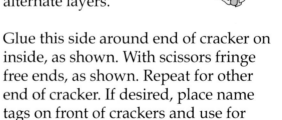

Glue this side around end of cracker on inside, as shown. With scissors fringe free ends, as shown. Repeat for other end of cracker. If desired, place name tags on front of crackers and use for party table setting.

Valentine Bags

Use small paper bags. Decorate one side of bag with crayons or paints. Add child's name.

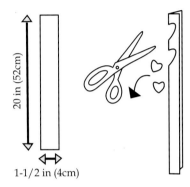

Cut paper strip 1-1/2 in x 20 in (4cm x 51cm). Fold in half lengthwise and cut out hearts or other patterns along the folded side and color.

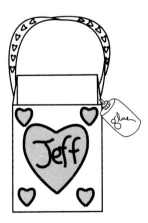

Glue one end to each side of bag. Suitable to hold Valentine or birthday party treats.

Party Hats
Helmet

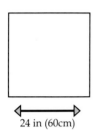 

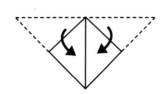

Cut a 24 in (60cm) square from a brown paper grocery bag. Fold in half diagonally.

Lay flat with the fold to the top. Bring the outside points to the middle, from the center of the folded side, and then

fold them back up. Fold them open to the sides like little wings. You have a diamond shape.

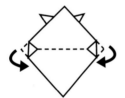 

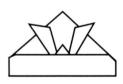

Fold one of the bottom sheets up half way. Then fold it up again.

Turn the helmet over and fold the left and the right tips of the folded bottom sheet,

around to the back. Fold the lower sheet upward. Crease well. Paint.

Head Fringe

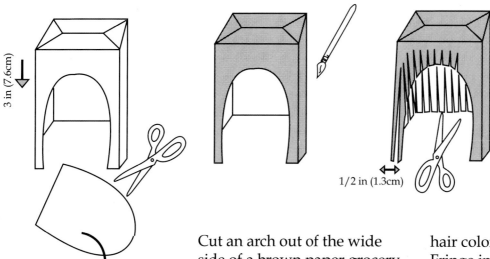

Cut an arch out of the wide side of a brown paper grocery bag to within 3 in (7.6cm) of the base of the bag. Paint it the hair color desired. Shellac. Fringe into strips 1/2 in (1.3cm) wide all around bag. Do not cut into base of bag.

Paperweight

Cut a piece of cardboard tube 3 in (7.6cm) long. Stand on brown paper and a layer of decorative paper as shown. Trace around tube end. Cut out the circles 3/4 in (2cm) larger than the traced circles.

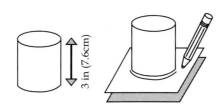

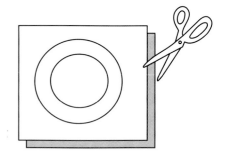

Make cuts around the enlarged edge of the circles and glue tabs to the end of tube, decorative paper on top, folding tabs down and gluing to sides of tabs.

Paperweight continued

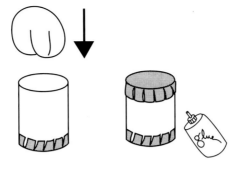

Turn tube over, place weight in tube, and repeat procedure to cover other end.

Cut a contrasting piece of paper as wide as the tube is long and long enough to wrap around the tube. Glue around tube. Tie a ribbon around tube.

Halloween Decorations
Ghost

Stuff a paper bag 1/2 full with crumpled newspaper. *Note* Light-weight bags and tissue paper stuffing should be used if you are ·making a mobile ghost. Gather top together for the neck and tape closed. Spread out the open end and cut 3 or 4 slits. This is ghost's body. Paint bag white. Add black eyes and mouth.

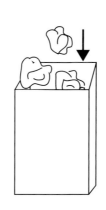

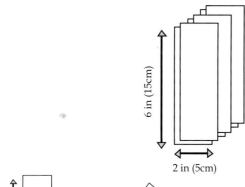

6 in (15cm)

2 in (5cm)

Cut strips of brown paper bags, each 6 in x 2 in (15cm x 5cm). Glue first strip in a circle. Link second strip in first and glue in a circle. Make chain 24 links long.

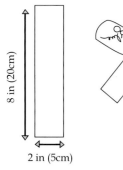

8 in (20cm)

2 in (5cm)

Cut another strip 8 in x 2 in (20cm x 5cm) for collar. Glue chain to collar.

Glue collar and chain around neck of ghost. Cut out a voice balloon 12 in x 8 in (30cm x 20cm), from cardboard. Paint white and allow to dry. Paint "BOO" on balloon and suspend near ghost's head.

Witch

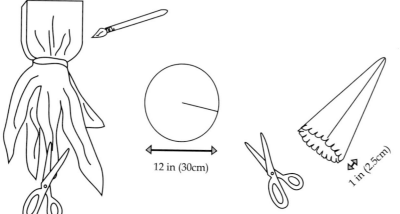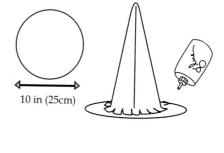

Stuff a large paper bag with crumpled newspaper 1/3 full for head. Gather top together and tape closed. Paint head green. Allow to dry. Spread out the open end of the bag and cut 3 or 4 slits. This is the witch body.

Draw a circle 12 in (30cm) in diameter from another paper bag. Slit it from one edge to the center point and lap over edges to make a cone. Glue.

Make 1-in (2.5-cm)-deep cuts around wide end of cone. Cut another circle 10 in (25cm) in diameter and glue the cone cut ends to it for a witch hat.

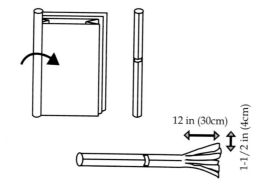

Glue the hat to the green head. Paint streamers and hat black. Paint black facial features on green head.

To make broomstick, use 3 large brown paper bags. Place one on top of the other and roll tightly from wide side. Tape closed. At one end of roll (don't choose bottom of bag), cut slits 12 in (30cm) long and 1–1/2 in (4cm) apart.

Spread the slits out for the broom's straw end. Glue the witch to the broom.

Stuffed Pumpkin

Stuff a large brown paper bag almost full with crumpled newspaper. Twist opening closed and tape. This is the stem. Cut 2 leaves from another paper bag. Cut a strip of brown paper 12 in x 4 in (30cm x 10cm).

  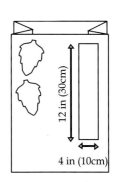

Spread the strip with glue on one side and twist for a vine. Glue the 2 leaves to vine and glue one end of vine to base of stem. Paint bag orange. Paint leaves, vine, and stem green.

Trick or Treat Bags
Pumpkin

 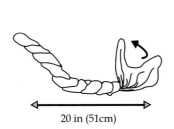 

Use a large brown paper grocery bag. Fold top down to the inside 8 in (20cm) and glue.

Paint bag orange for a pumpkin. Add a jack-o-lantern face with black paint. Twist a green plastic bag into a handle, 20 in

(51cm) long, staple ends to the narrow sides of the painted bag.

Cat

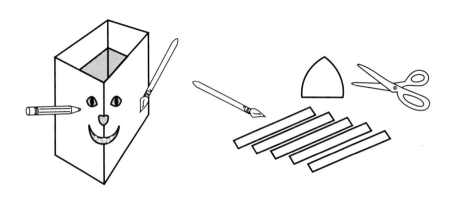

Prepare the paper bag as for the pumpkin (p63). Make cat face on corner of bag with black crayon, as shown.

Color in green eyes, red nose, and pink mouth with white teeth. Cut out 2 paper ears and 6 paper whiskers and

paint black. Allow to dry. Glue to face. Paint the bag with black strokes for cat fur.

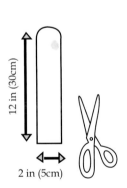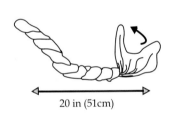

12 in (30cm)

2 in (5cm)

20 in (51cm)

Cut a strip of paper from another bag about 2 in x 12 in (5cm x 30cm), with one end rounded. Paint black.

Allow to dry. Curl this tail around your finger and glue straight end to the bag. Twist a black plastic bag into a

handle 20 in (51cm) long, and staple ends to the narrow sides of the painted bag.

Horn of Plenty

Use a medium brown paper bag. Fold back 1 in (2.5cm) around the open end. Press down and fold again, to make a rim.

Cut the bottom out of the bag. Make 4 slits 6 in (15cm) along the folds on the 4 corners of the bag, as shown.

6 in (15cm)

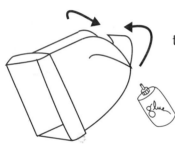

Overlap and glue until the bag comes to a point. Twist the pointed end and curl it slightly.

With brown paint, make rows of the letter "s" all over the bag for a basket effect.

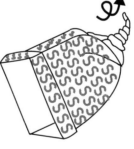

Loosely stuff small paper bags with crumpled newspaper. Fold in ends and tape. Shape bags to resemble fruits and vegetables. Bananas and cobs of corn work well. Paint the fruits appropriate colors. When dry, glue into open end of horn.

Autumn Table Setting

Place Mats

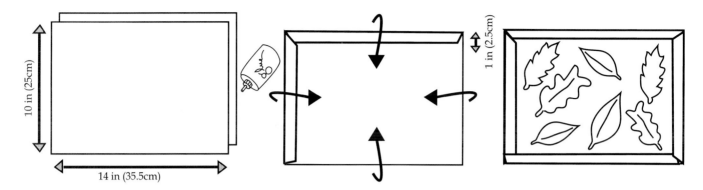

Cut open a brown paper bag. Cut 2 sheets 14 in x 10 in (35.5cm x 25cm).

Glue one on top of the other. Fold over 1 in (2.5cm) edge on all sides. Glue down.

This makes top border. Paint. Glue autumn leaves on surface for decoration. Shellac.

Napkin Rings

Cut a ring 1–1/2 in (4cm) wide off end of cardboard tube. Cut strips of yellow crepe paper 3 in x 6 in long (8cm x 15cm). Wrap around ring and glue in place, as shown. Cover ring.

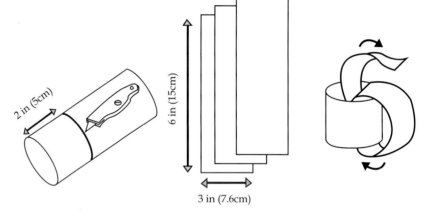

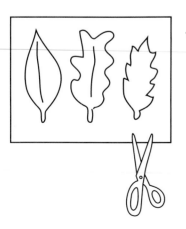

Glue autumn leaves on piece of brown paper. Cut out around leaf. Glue to napkin ring, as shown.

Turkey Centerpiece

 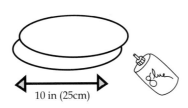 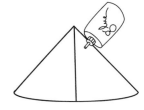

Stuff a medium brown paper bag with crumpled newspaper and tape shut. Using another brown paper bag, cut 2 circles, 10 in (25cm) in diameter. Glue together, one on top of the other. Cut another circle, 4 in (10cm) in diameter. Cut from the edge to the center point of the small circle and overlap ends into a cone shape.

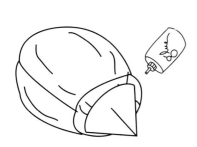  

Glue along overlapped ends. This cone is the turkey's beak. Paint yellow. Allow to dry. Glue over the taped end of the stuffed bag, as shown.

Cut the other circle in half and glue, curved part pointing up, to other end of bag for the tail. Cut the other half circle in half again to make

2 quarter circles. Glue one to each side of the stuffed bag, curved part pointing downward, for the wings on the turkey. Paint yellow and black eyes.

 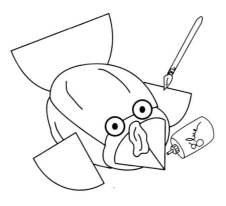

Paint the body of the turkey with black strokes for feathers. Paint head red. Make wattle, as shown, from small piece of brown paper. Paint red and glue to top of head.

Totem Pole

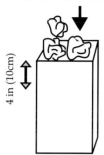

smaller top bag for head

Stuff 3 brown paper grocery bags with crumpled newspaper, pressing it in tightly. Leave 4 in (10cm) unstuffed at the top of the bag. Fold the brown paper over and glue the opening shut. Tape. Stuff another grocery bag 3/4 full with crumpled newspaper. Make cuts in the sides of the bag down to the newspapers, as shown.

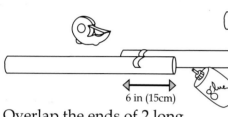

Overlap the ends of 2 long cardboard tubes about 6 in (15cm). Glue and tape. Place the overlapped section in the middle of the bag. Add more crumpled newspaper around the tubes to make a level bottom and fold the brown paper down over the paper and tubes. Glue in place. Turn bag over. Glue a toilet tissue tube to the top of the bag.

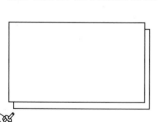
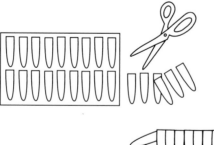

Cut out bottoms of 2 grocery bags, cut bags open and lay flat. Spread glue over one sheet and smooth the other sheet over it. From this paper cut out feather shapes, and glue these to the cardboard tube on the top, and on the tube wings, as shown. Paint to resemble a parrot (see photo) and shellac. Paint animal faces on other 3 bags. Cut out ears from the double layered bag for the animal head bags and glue, as shown. Shellac. Stack one on top of the other and glue together.

70

Snowman

  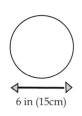 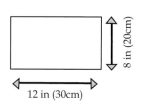

Stuff a large brown paper grocery bag loosely with crumpled newspaper. Tape the top shut. Allow part of bag for head. Squeeze together at "neck" and tape well. Tie with

a colored scarf made from a strip of colored plastic bag. Paint snowman white. Paint orange carrot nose on face and orange and black eyes and buttons down the front.

Cut a 6 in (15cm) circle from a paper bag. Cut a rectangle 8 in wide by 12 in long (20cm x 30cm). Roll into cylinder, short ends together, and glue.

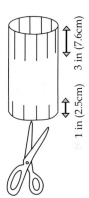 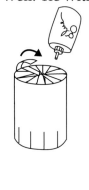  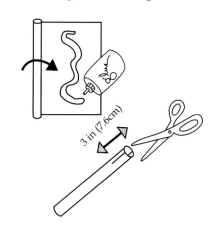

Make 1 in (2.5cm) cuts around one end of cylinder and 3 in (7.6cm) cuts around the other end. Fold 3 in (7.6cm) tabs over and glue one on top of the other.

Fold 1 in (2.5cm) tabs outward and glue onto 6 in (15cm) circle. Glue this hat to top of snowman. Paint black.

Make arms by cutting end out of long paper bag. Spread glue on one side, and roll into a tube, glued side inward. Make a cut 3 in (7.6cm) long in one end of tube.

Twist tube into stick with forked end. Repeat for other stick. Make 1 in (2.5cm) cut on each side of bag. Spread glue on end of arm and insert in cut.

Christmas
Table
Setting

Angel with Horn

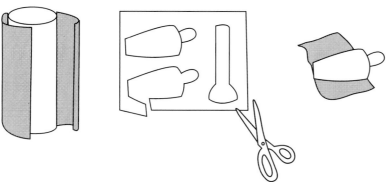

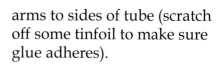

Cover a toilet tissue tube with tinfoil. Cut out 2 arms with hands from thin cardboard. Cover arms with silver foil.

Cut out horn from cardboard and cover with gold foil. Glue hands of both arms to the horn and other ends of

arms to sides of tube (scratch off some tinfoil to make sure glue adheres).

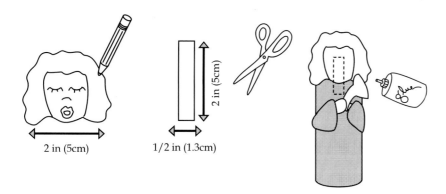

On cardboard draw and cut out angel head with hair, 2 in (5cm) across. Cut a strip of cardboard 1/2 in x 2 in (1.3cm x 5cm).

Glue one end of strip to back of angel head and other end to inside of tube, so head overlaps, as shown. Paint face, hair, and hands.

Glue a circle of gold foil to back of head for halo. Glue paper doily to back of angel for wings. Make 2 for the choir.

Santa Claus

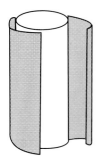 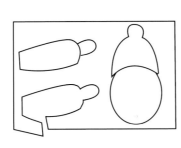 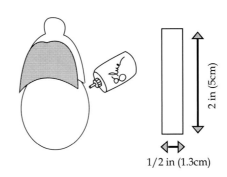

Cover a toilet tissue tube with red paper, as for angel. Glue edges, tuck ends in. Cut 2 arms with hands. Cover arms with red paper. Glue on

paper. Draw and cut out from cardboard a head with a hat. Cover hat with red paper. Glue on.

Cut a strip of cardboard 1/2 in x 2 in (1.3cm x 5cm).

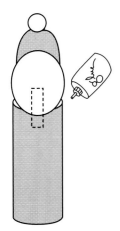 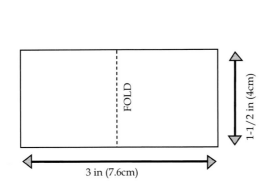 

Glue one end of strip to back of Santa head and other end to inside of tube.

Cut out 3 in x 1–1/2 in (7.5cm x 4cm) song book from thin cardboard. Fold in half.

Unfold and glue hands to sides of book and arms to sides of tube. Paint hands, book, and face. Glue on cotton batting for beard, hair, and hat.

Drummer Boy

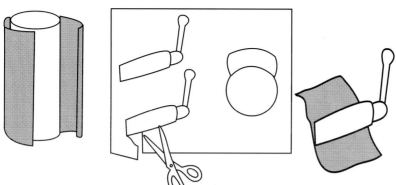

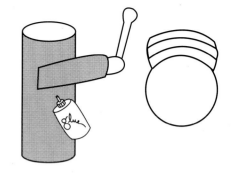

Cover a toilet tissue tube with blue paper, as for angel and Santa Claus. Glue edges, tuck ends in. Cut 2 arms with hands and drum sticks from thin cardboard. Cover arms with blue paper. Glue on. Draw and cut out a head with pill box hat from thin cardboard. Cut out 1/2 in by 2 in (1.3cm x 5cm) cardboard strip.

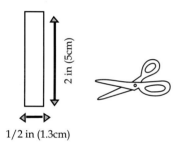

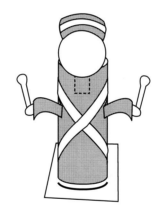

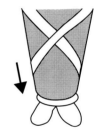

Glue one end of strip to back of head and other end to inside of tube, so head overlaps, as shown.

Cover hat with blue paper. Cut 2 strips of yellow paper 1/2 in x 6 in (1.3cm x 15cm) and glue across front of body cylinder in an "X."

Cut out another yellow strip 1/4 in (.6cm) wide and glue around top of hat.

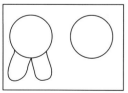

Cut 1–1/2 in (4cm) ring from end of another toilet tissue tube for drum. Place cylinder flat on thin cardboard. Trace twice, making 2 circles.

Draw feet out from one circle and cut out. Glue to bottom of body cylinder. Cut out other cardboard circle and glue to top of drum. Glue drum to front of body cylinder. Paint drum, drumstick, hands, face, and feet.

Place Mats

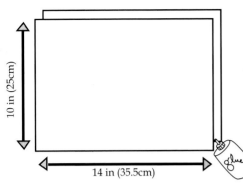

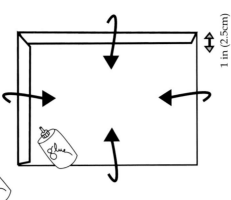

Cut open a brown paper bag. Cut 2 sheets 14 in x 10 in (35.5cm x 25cm). Glue one on top of the other. Fold over 1 in (2.5cm) edge on all sides. Glue down. This makes top border. Paint.

Glue 1/4 in (.6cm) Christmas ribbon around border. Glue holly leaves on surface for decoration. Shellac.

Napkin Rings

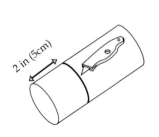

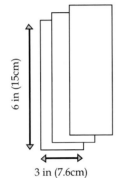

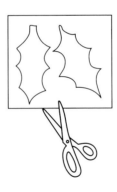

Cut cardboard tube into 2 in (5cm) slices. Paint or cover each ring with colored crepe paper, cloth, or wrap with 2 in (5cm) wide velvet ribbon. Glue ends. Decorate for the occasion with tiny flowers, holly leaves, ribbons, or the names of dinner guests.

Crackers

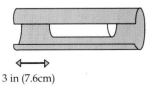

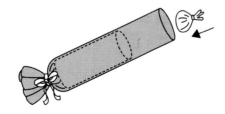

Cover toilet tissue tubes with crepe paper in Christmas colors. Tape edges. Allow the covering paper to extend 3 in (7.6cm) beyond each end of the tube. Tie one end of the paper with colored wool or ribbon. Fill the tube with treats, wrapped candy, balloons, small toys. Twist and tie the paper shut at this end. Decorate with Christmas seals or glue and sparkles. Put place names on crackers, if you wish.

Index